God Waited for Me

Dawn Brown

©Copyright 2024 Dawn Brown

All rights reserved. This book is protected under the copyright laws of the United States of America.

ISBN-13: 978-1-954609-59-4

No portion of this book may be reproduced, distributed, or transmitted in any form, including photocopying, recording, or other electronic or mechanical methods, without the written permission of the publisher, except in the case of brief quotations embodied in reviews and certain other non-commercial uses permitted by copyright law. Permission granted on request.

For information regarding special discounts for bulk purchases contact the Publisher:

LaBoo Publishing Enterprise, LLC
staff@laboopublishing.com

Dedication

I dedicate this book to my husband Michael, children Dionysia, Diona, and Michael Jr., mom Cecelia Campbell, dad, Willie Campbell Jr., brothers Alex and Willie Jr., sisters Yvette, Cecelia, and Renee, best friend Bridgett Patten, in-laws Joseph, Delcie, Terrance, and Pamela Brown, nieces and nephews, Antoine, Renata, Brendon, Sharnell, and Alex, Jr., and friends for all their prayers and support, as well as to the doctors and nurses, Marsha, Taneara, and Michelle, at the Baltimore VA Hospital who cared for me over the years and saved my life. Without all of you, how I handled my many illnesses and hospital stays would have been completely different.

Table of Contents

Introduction.................................1

Growing Up.................................3

In the Navy.................................7

Isn't She Lovely...........................17

Hodgkin's Disease.........................23

A Close Call...............................29

Chemotherapy.............................33

My Dad's Last Year........................35

Meeting My Husband.....................39

Tremors....................................43

Kidney Issues and Breast Cancer..........47

Kidney Failure.............................55

Hysterectomy..............................61

Dialysis Grafts, Catheters, and Fistulas 63

Travel 67

God Answers 71

Panic Attacks 75

COVID 79

Death Came Calling. 83

Introduction

In this story you will meet Dawn, a woman whose life has been turned upside down by one health issue after another. It doesn't stop her from continuing to live. She remains happy through it all. She could have sat back and wallowed in self-pity, but she refused. There was and still is too much out there in nature that she wants to see and experience. Her hope is that when you finish reading her story, you know that having an illness does not mean your life is over and you have to stop living. Start by doing the little things that make you happy and go from there. Appreciate your life and what you have in it. Things get rough and we want to feel sorry for ourselves. It doesn't have to be that way. Make the best of every day. Start crossing things off your bucket list. Take pictures so that you can look back on them and smile. Enjoy life.

Growing Up

I know you've seen on television when people win awards, they begin their acceptance speeches with, "I want to give glory and honor to God…" Well, I want to say the same thing. If it had not been for Him…

I grew up just like most children, thinking about my future. At one time, I wanted to work with animals. I changed my mind after receiving a Navy book cover from my mom in junior high school, and I decided I wanted to join. I thought it would be easy. I would see the world and then retire. Well, God had other plans for my life.

I was born on Broadway Avenue in Baltimore. I have two brothers, Willie and Alex, and three sisters, Yvette, Cecelia, and Renee. I don't remember much of our time there. I do remember when we moved to Belgin Avenue. I have two memories while living there. One was my sisters and the boys up the street throwing rocks at each other. A rock hit my brother, Willie, on the head. My sisters told my mom that one of the boys threw the rock, but it was one of my sisters.

The other memory was of my mom pouring water out of the window to separate our dog and a dog from up the street. When I was four years old, we moved to Oakley Avenue. My first memory was going into our empty bedroom and seeing a tennis ball lying on the floor.

Next thing I knew, the school year started. I cried as I watched my brothers and sisters leave for school and I couldn't go because I was too young. Once I started, I only missed one day. I loved receiving perfect attendance awards. I never really got sick except when I suffered from tonsillitis. When I was 14, the doctor told my mom if she brought me in again for it, I would have to have my tonsils removed. Two weeks later they swelled up. I was scheduled for a tonsillectomy. I got excited, thinking I was going to be able to eat all the ice cream I wanted. I was mistaken. The nurse said, "Aww. She's afraid to talk." They gave me Italian ice. I told my mom it burned but she continued to give it to me.

A year later I felt a lump in my breast. I didn't tell my mom. I went to the school doctor. He felt the lump. He told me to eat bran and he would see me back in a couple of weeks. I talked to the priest at church and was told I needed to tell my mom. I talked to my friends at church. We gathered in a room, and they prayed over me. Two weeks later the doctor called for me. My teacher asked me why he wanted to see me. I told her that I didn't know. It didn't dawn on me that he wanted to recheck me. She didn't want to let me go but had no choice. The doctor checked me, and the lump was gone. He asked if I had eaten the bran and I told him no. I told him that my friends at church prayed over me. That was my first healing from God.

I consider myself to have had a blessed childhood. Every summer, my mom and dad took us on outings. My mom would wake us up and tell us to shower and get dressed. Smelling the fried chicken, we knew we were going on a trip. Our favorite Motown songs would play. Renee, Willie, Alex, and I even made up a song about the checkerboard squares on the water tower that we always passed. We went to the Smithsonian Museum in Washington, DC and the zoo there. Wildwood, New Jersey and Hershey Park in Pennsylvania were our favorites. We went to Busch Gardens in Virginia and Tampa, before they had rides. I remember going into the House of Frankenstein in Wildwood. It was scary and fun at the same time. Frankenstein would always chase us back to the entrance. He always remembered my sister for some strange reason. One year he told her to be quiet and let her pass. He chased everyone else back to the entrance. My dad always found a prime parking spot right at the boardwalk. All the children in the neighborhood were envious. Sometimes we would take one of our cousins or the girl across the street with us. My dad drove the family to Disney World in 1973 in our green station wagon. When we arrived in Florida, there were orange juice stands along the road. My dad got out of the car to get a sample. We watched him take the sips, making the sound "ahh" and smiling. After a few sips, he finally let us get out of the car and he laughed.

One summer, my mom and dad took Renee and I to Georgia and Walt Disney World. To our surprise, my dad road Space Mountain with us. Mom and Dad would usually send us kids on our way and they would just walk around the parks. While in the Haunted Mansion, I reached around to the car that my mom and dad were riding in and touched my dad. He screamed so loud. That was the first time I had ever seen my dad scared. Renee and I laughed so hard.

Fast forward to 12th grade: My mom took me to the doctor because I was having problems with the circulation in my hands. When my hands were exposed to the air, they would turn blue. I was sent to see a vascular doctor. I walked into the office, and everyone stared at me. No wonder—all the patients looked to be over seventy, or that's what I thought looking at all the white hair. The doctor had me wear gloves until they could figure out what was wrong. Unfortunately, I had to go to school this way. Sitting in my English class, my teacher noticed that I was wearing gloves. She told me to take them off. My friend Mitzi explained to her that if I took them off my hands would turn blue. My teacher didn't believe it and told me to take them off. I took them off and my hands turned blue. The teacher panicked and told me to hurry up and put them back on. The doctor was never able to figure out why. It just went away on its own.

In the spring I walked in the March of Dimes walkathon. By the time I finished the walk my left shoulder had swollen and I couldn't turn my head. I was taken to the hospital by ambulance and given no diagnosis, just a neck brace to wear for two weeks.

In the Navy

In August 1982 I joined the Navy. At the Navy Recruit Training Command Orlando, FL we were issued our uniforms in boot camp. Everything was put into one giant duffel bag. We had to march back to the barracks with the duffel bag on our backs. By the time we got there my left shoulder had swelled up again and I couldn't turn my head. My Company Commander (CC) would not send me to Medical. The next day I went to class in extreme pain. Watching me cry, the instructor was hesitant about sending me because my CC didn't send me. By the end of the day, I was finally sent to Medical. Again, there was no diagnosis but I was put in a neck brace once again and given pain pills. I wore the brace for two weeks. I had to go back to see the doctor and was sent to physical therapy for six weeks. Boot camp was only eight weeks, and we were in week two. At week eight, the doctor asked me if I wanted to go back to my company or be put behind two weeks because I needed more therapy, which meant I couldn't graduate with my company. I chose to go back. I was determined to pass the physical fitness test so that I could graduate with them. We had to run twenty-two laps to pass. Everyone cheered me on so I could finish. Some even ran extra laps with me to encourage me. I finished and graduated with my company.

I went to "A" school in Meridian, Mississippi for six weeks. There you are taught about your Rate or, as Army folk say, MOS. We went to normal classes. At the end of each day, we had free time. I would go to the gym and work out. One day, I decided I would leg press 180 lbs. I made a big mistake. Don't get me wrong, I was able to do it—several times, even. I paid for it later. I pulled all the muscles in my back. I recovered after a week of muscle relaxers. At the end of school, we could choose our duty station by picking two places we would like to be stationed. My first choice was Hawaii. My second was Italy. There were only two females in my class. Our orders came in separately from the males. Hers was the other way around. We were excited and couldn't wait to hear. The choices were repair ships out of Hawaii and Italy. I was so happy. She told me that I could choose first. I picked Hawaii and so she got Italy. I only picked Hawaii so my mom could come to see me there. She always wanted to go to Hawaii, and now she had a reason.

After "A" school I got to go home for a month. When my month was over, I took a bus to Dallas/Ft. Worth airport to catch a seven-hour flight to Honolulu, Hawaii. There were only 10 of us on this big 747 plane. I asked the stewardess where everyone else was. She said, "This is it." I was terrified.

In the Navy

I wouldn't put my window shade down. They started playing a movie. The stewardess told me that I had to put the shade down. I told her that if the plane went down, I wanted to see it before it hit the ground. Before I left to go into the military, I had won a stuffed dog that I had named Paul. I named him after a guy I liked who worked at my summer job. I took Paul with me on the plane. I even strapped him into a seat. The captain came out later and asked if I had paid for a seat for him and laughed.

When I arrived in Hawaii, I was so happy to get off the plane. One of my shipmates met me at the airport. I was terrified and excited at the same time. I arrived at the ship to a bunch of stares. One guy just watched me the whole time. I found out later his name was Frank. After I'd been aboard for some time, he decided he wanted to show me the island. We dated for about six months, then he got out of the Navy.

The island was beautiful: water views all around, sun rays in the valleys. It was amazing. My duty station was aboard The USS *Jason* AR-8 in Pearl Harbor. I was a Ship's Serviceman. We operated the laundry, dry cleaners, ship's stores, barbershops, and vending machines. I started my career working in the laundry. We washed, dried, and sometimes folded the crew's laundry. We pressed uniforms for E-7s and above, which included officers. There were two stores on board, one for uniforms, toiletries, electronics, jewelry, etc., and the other, called "The Gedunk," for junk food. I never knew what that meant. I also got to run both stores. We had two barbershops:

one for the officers and the other for the enlisted. I never got to cut hair. I was chosen as an E-3 to work in the Gedunk. In the ship's history, no one below an E-4 had ever worked in any of the stores. I loved it. The crew loved me.

The ship went on what was called a WestPac, which is a Western Pacific cruise. We traveled to the Philippines. I went on a tour to Villa Escudero, where I stayed in a hut and dined at the foot of a waterfall with the water running over my feet. In Yokosuka, Japan, I went out with a group of friends to a Chinese restaurant. I ordered egg foo young, not knowing it was nothing like the way it is made in the United States, and egg rolls. They brought me three plates: one with eggs, one with rice, and one piled with egg rolls—no gravy like we eat in the US. In Hong Kong, we dined in the floating restaurant that you saw in the series Shogun. Singapore was the cleanest city I have ever seen. In Busan, Korea, which we called Pusan, we went shopping in the marketplace. A man decided it was okay to put his hand on my butt. My friends had to pick me up and carry me out of the store to keep me from slapping him and then getting into trouble for fighting. We went to the Comoros Islands, where my shipmates built houses for the people and watched them slaughter a bull. They had a wonderful party for us. We walked to the hotel where the party was, and I felt like we were celebrities. The people lined the streets. They parted like the Red Sea to let us into the hotel and then stood in the windows to watch us. On our next cruise, the captain was given a choice of anchoring out at sea or going to Australia. He chose to anchor twelve miles from land in the Indian Ocean. The scenery was beautiful. Never in my life had I expected to be on a ship, look down, and see a sea turtle. It was huge and beautiful. I was amazed. We also went to Guantanamo Bay, Cuba, Seoul, Korea, and Guam.

I got to cross the equator twice, once as a slimy Pollywog. We had to undergo a Shellback initiation, or Line Crossing Ceremony. They woke us up very early in the morning. We had to put our clothes on inside out and backwards. We were fed green eggs from a plate on the floor but we could not use our hands to eat. We had to crawl around on our knees throughout the ship while being chased by those already Shellbacks, of which there weren't many. Most of the crew were Pollywogs. In the end we had to crawl through a tube of trash that they tried to save for a week, but it kept getting tossed overboard. We rolled in a homemade coffin of trash. Most of it was gone by the time I got in. We had to put our faces in the Royal Baby's belly, which was covered with whipped cream to retrieve a cherry. Then we were dubbed Shellbacks by King Neptune aka the Captain. Afterwards, everyone was so tired that we got to relax for the rest of the day. The next day we celebrated with a cookout on the boat deck. On the second crossing, I was a shellback. There were very few pollywogs because only a few sailors had reported for duty after the initial crossing.

After my round of working in the Gedunk for three months, I was sent to work on the mess decks. All E-3 and below had to make at least one ninety-day tour of working on the mess deck, which is the cafeteria. I was serving lunch one day and the Supply Officer came to me and told me that I was going back to work in the Gedunk. I asked him why. He said, "Because the crew requested you. You must finish your tour first."

One Saturday we had a working party, when a group of us would receive stores (resaleable goods) or supplies. I threw a box of plastic bags on the floor. The Mess Deck's Master-At-Arms (MDMAA), which is like a security guard, began yelling at me about dropping the box. I told him that it was just plastic bags. He kept yelling, telling me to pick the box up and put it down gently. I walked up to him later and told him that he made black people look bad. He cried. Quick backstory: He yelled at anyone just walking across the mess decks and would say, "This is my mess deck; I can do what I want. I'm the law." All the black people disliked him. No others in a position of power had behaved that way. He was the first and only black MDMAA during my tour. He spoke to one of the white Mess Management Specialists, who told him to write me up for a racial slur. The Division Officer for Mess Management called me in his office and told me that I needed to apologize. I did, with reluctance, after explaining to him that calling a black man black is not a racial slur. But that wasn't the end. I had to go to the Executive Officer's Inquiry (XOI), which would decide if I had to go to Captain's Mast. Captain's Mast is like going to court. Anyway, the XO asked me what happened. I told him and explained why I made the statement. The XO called the MDMAA in and asked if I had apologized. He told the XO no. The Division Officer stepped up and said, "Yes, she did." I was told to leave because the MDMAA was higher ranking than me and was not supposed to be chewed out in front of subordinates. The XO went off on him and told him that he had no business writing me up and that the next time he was asked a question he had better tell the truth. The MDMAA was ordered to apologize to me and told me what happened after I was sent out of the room. He was relieved of his duties.

I couldn't wait to go back to working in the Gedunk. Whenever we went out to sea, I would reopen the store in the evening for movie nights. When we returned to Pearl Harbor, I would open on Saturdays for a couple of hours for the people who had duty (stand watch) that day.

After being an E-3, we were required to take an advancement exam. I took my exam and failed. All my superiors were really upset about it, especially the Supply Officer. One day he came to my window and told me that after I finished this tour in the Gedunk, he wanted me to come work for him as his secretary. I went on leave while working for him and when I returned, he informed me that I had been nominated for advancement to E-4. He told me that they would not convene the board until I had returned from leave. When I was interviewed, I found out that I was the only E-3 who had been nominated. I was so nervous. When I was done with the interview, I left them laughing. Every time I would see one of the officers who sat on the board, they would congratulate me. Even the Commodore congratulated me. All of them said that they weren't supposed to say anything because the results had not been released yet. They announced it over the PA system. I was elated. The Supply Officer called my mom. She thought something had happened to me. She and my dad were so proud. I received Sailor of the Quarter Award for my Division and department several times over the course of my tour aboard.

I had a habit of rushing through the ship and one day I jumped through a hatch (doorway) and hit my shin. I sustained a bruise so bad that it traveled down my leg into my foot. I went to Medical. I was put on four days' bedrest to avoid a clot. I was allowed to stay in a hotel in Waikiki. My friends came after work with food.

After working for the Supply Officer, I went to work in the Ship's Store. We went on a second WestPac. Kris Kristofferson came to perform for the crew. Because I was working in the store, I couldn't go to the show. He asked if he could come down to see me. I was in shock. He said that he was told that I was preparing for inventory and couldn't come up, so he came down. He gave me an autograph and took a picture with me.

That night we did inventory. We added up the sales for that day, and they totaled $9,999.75. My Division Officer was so happy that she asked if anyone had a quarter to make it an even $10,000. That was the highest single day sales in the history of the ship up to that time. Our profits from the stores were donated to Morale, Welfare and Recreation for the crew. During my tours in the stores, I generated the most profits ever until I transferred. I'm not sure if my record was ever broken.

Beginning in 1984 and throughout my military career blood was found in my urine and I was sent to the hospital for additional blood tests, with each doctor telling me that I needed a kidney biopsy. That didn't happen, and there was no explanation why.

Isn't She Lovely

My next duty station was another ship stationed in Norfolk, VA, the USS Emory S. Land AS-39. I moved into an apartment with no furniture. I had to request advance pay to get some. All I could do was study. I had to take the advancement exam and passed soon after I got aboard and was advanced to E-5. After my tour was up, I transferred to shore duty and worked at the Norfolk Commissary.

I became pregnant while working there. I never let my pregnancy stop me from doing my job. At that time, I worked in the warehouse. I still moved pallets, put cases of seltzer water on the shelves, drove the forklifts, and mopped the entire warehouse. The only thing I couldn't do was go into the freezer for an extended period. My abdomen would cramp up. During the sixth month of my pregnancy, I woke up and my face, hands, and feet were swollen. I didn't recognize myself. I went to the doctor, and she told me that I had to go on bed rest. I asked her for how long. She said, "Until you have the baby." I went back to the Commissary and told them what she said. After that, I went home. I stayed at home and only went out to buy food and go to my doctor's appointments.

In August 1988 I got my driver's license and in November I had my first child. I was determined not to catch a bus with a baby, so I bought my first car. I was due October 23rd. I went to the hospital on Friday, November 13th, thinking I was in labor. They sent me home. I went back again on Monday. I had my friend Mary follow me. The doctors had me walk the floor for two hours (this was supposed to help dilate me). It didn't. I was sent home. I told Mary I didn't need her to stay with me. I got in the shower and the contractions got so strong that I barely made it out. I couldn't get dressed after I got out of the shower. I called Mary back and told her I needed to go back to the hospital. The nurse kept telling me I wasn't dilated enough. I received an epidural. After being there a while, I told the nurse that the baby was coming. She told me that I couldn't go into the delivery room until I was able to move my legs. Again, I told her my baby was ready to come. She repeated her comment about my legs and said they weren't putting them up in the stirrups for me. I told her that I would have it right where I was. The doctor came in to check me. He said, "She's crowning." I was rushed to the delivery room. They bumped into every doorway and wall on the way. The doctor asked me if I would mind if some med students came in. I said no. There were twenty people in the room when Dionysia was born. She arrived on November 15. Three pushes—that's all it took. She became the commissary baby. Everyone loved her.

Isn't She Lovely

In 1990, I transferred to the USS Yosemite AD-19, a ship in Mayport, FL. The ship departed in October of 1991 for a MedCruise (Mediterranean Cruise). Dee stayed with my mom and dad in Baltimore. As the ship was leaving Italy, I discovered that I was pregnant, as was another young lady. The disbursing officer threw money overboard to us because we didn't have any and they had already moved the brow and told us to go to the base to be sent back to Mayport. We weren't allowed to be onboard while pregnant.

Our flight back to the States was delayed. We were put up in a hotel for the night. They served all of us dinner. It looked delicious. I started moving my rice around my plate and to my surprise, I saw a tentacle. My stomach turned. I told the waiter that I could not eat it and to remove it from in front of me or else I would get sick. He brought the restaurant manager out and I was asked if I liked spaghetti. I told him yes and they fixed it for me. I was so happy. The others at the table said it wasn't fair. He explained that I was pregnant. It took two days to get back to Florida because we had missed our flight by the time we got to Philadelphia.

This was not an easy pregnancy. The muscles in my back would not stretch. I was in constant pain when standing or walking. At fourteen weeks, I was put on bedrest. She wouldn't grow. After my amniocentesis the doctors told me that she might have spina bifida because they saw a spot on her abdomen that they thought might be a hole. They told me I had to make the heart-wrenching decision whether to keep her or abort her. I was told that I had a week to decide if the results came back positive. I was devastated. The results were negative, thank God. She continued to have problems. There wasn't enough fluid around her. She still wasn't growing. I was put on baby aspirin. I prayed and asked God to make my baby okay. About a month later her growth spurted, and the fluid increased. My prayers were answered, and I was so grateful. On the morning of July 2nd my water broke. I called the sitter, drove into Mayport to drop off Dee, and drove to Baptist Medical Center in Jacksonville. At 4:12 my second baby girl, Diona, was born. She was born a week earlier than her due date and weighed six pounds, five ounces. My little girl was healthy. Now I had two children while in the Navy on my own: Dionysia, whose nickname was Dee but was sometimes called Yoda (when she turned to the side, she looked just like him), and Diona, who I called "Chuck E" because she loved "Chuck E. Cheese" restaurant. I eventually left Mayport and transferred to a ship out of Norfolk, the USS Shenandoah AD-44. While stationed there, I went on another Med-Cruise. This time, I made the whole cruise. We went to Italy, Greece, Spain, and the United Arab Emirates, where I went on a tour to Israel. I went to the Wailing Wall and was so overcome with emotion that I could not stop crying. I was having problems with my legs, so I walked into the Jordan River and I had no more problems. After we returned, I was in a car accident where I totaled my car. The car flipped over, hit the driver's side roof on the ground and landed upright. The firemen had to pry the door open to get me out. They told me that I should not have been able to walk away from it. I escaped with a mild concussion and bruised ribs. BUT GOD!!!

Hodgkin's Disease

One night, I was sitting in a restaurant with one of my shipmates, when I suddenly got a severe pain in my hip. She took me to Portsmouth Naval Hospital. The doctor told me that I had an infection and the ship's doctor would have to figure out what it was. While out at sea I was working in the laundry and developed chest pains. I was kept in Medical for a few days. Upon our return, they sent me to the base clinic for a chest x-ray and I was told nothing. Six months later there was a request to repeat the x-ray. During those six months, I developed severe pain in my lower back, to the point of almost not being able to walk. I would sit down and the next thing you know, I was asleep. One of my shipmates was astonished that when he walked out of the room I had been laughing hysterically and when he came back seconds later, I was asleep. I kept going to Medical because the pain was excruciating. They gave me Motrin and Percocet. While sitting outside their door on one visit, I just happened to look up at my record and saw that the x-ray showed a mass in my chest which no one told me about. I was angry. The doctor said I couldn't participate in the physical fitness test because of my back. One of the other female first class in my division told her that I was faking to get out of the test, so the doctor just kept giving me pain meds that didn't work. I struggled to get from my car to the ship every morning. It took thirty minutes to make a ten-minute trip. Walking up the stairs was horrible. One day the Supply Officer was coming up the stairs behind me and asked, "Why are you still on board?" I said, "Every time I go to Medical, they just give me pain pills that don't work." He said, "Go in the office and wait until I come back." He came back with transfer papers and told me to get my things and get off the ship. I found out later, after I was taken off the ship, that he cussed the doctor out for not having taken me off sooner.

I was sent to Medical Hold, where military personnel went when they had medical issues that prevented them from staying with their commands. I had a bone scan from head to toe and was told there were pools of blood in my lower spine and my head. During that time, I saw an Internal Medicine doctor who could not figure out what was wrong with me. She talked to several doctors in the hospital about my case. They told her she needed to admit me. The doctor explained to them that I had two little children and I needed to make arrangements for someone to take care of them while I was in the hospital. I talked to my babysitter, and she agreed to keep them.

During all of this, I had been trying to get Dee into a school in Portsmouth where my babysitter lived and was told she had to go in the city where I lived, which was Chesapeake. Even after explaining that I was in the military and had to be to work at 6 am, it didn't matter. I was beside myself in disbelief. They expected me to leave a six-year-old at home by herself to wait for the bus to pick her up. So I did the only thing I could do: I sent her back to Baltimore with my parents to start school. After being tested, Dee was put in the first grade.

When I went back to see the doctor, she said, "I'm admitting you to the cancer ward. It doesn't mean you have cancer. It's just the only place I could get a bed." So I was admitted. While at the hospital I had an MRI. I was in the chamber for two hours. I also had a CAT scan and a biopsy. I was then sent to an oncologist.

He said, "You have cancer. It's called Hodgkin's disease. You are in Stage IV. It's in your lymphatic system and has spread to your lungs. The largest tumor is in your chest. You have a large one on your spine. Where are you from?"

I said, "Baltimore."

He said, "We are going to send you back there for treatment. You need to move in with your parents because you won't be able to take care of your children by yourself."

Dread came over me. The one person I hated to give the news to was my mom. I was afraid to tell her because I knew it would break her heart. She had lost her best friend to cancer a couple of years before that. I finally called her.

I said, "Mom, sit down. I have something to tell you."

She said, "Why do I need to sit down? What's wrong?"

I said, "I have cancer."

She said, "What do you mean you have cancer?"

I told her, "It's called Hodgkin's disease. They are going to treat me at the National Naval Medical Center (NNMC) in Bethesda. The doctor said that if I had to have cancer this is the one to have. It has the highest cure rate. He said I needed to come home because I wouldn't be able to care for Dee and Diona by myself."

So back to Baltimore I went. Dee was shocked and so happy to see us.

I met with the doctors at NNMC, now known as Walter Reed National Military Medical Center. One after another they came into the room and asked if I wanted any more children. I told them no. When the last one came in, I asked why they kept asking that question. I was told that chemo can make you sterile. The doctor handed me a list of the drugs that would be used to treat me and their side effects. They could cause damage to all of the systems in my body. I said, "So I can be cured of cancer and die because of the damage the chemo did to my heart?" The irony… He said, "Yes." I asked to be left alone to think about it. My thoughts were that I couldn't leave my daughters. I agreed to go through it for my daughters and my mom.

I went in to have a catheter placed in my chest. The next day I called my doctor because I was having severe pain in my arm, and it was swelling. He had me come in and sent me for an ultrasound. When I got back to his office, he said, "I called your mother and told her that if you showed up at home, she needed to bring you back immediately. I am admitting you. You have a blood clot in your arm."

I was upset. During my admission, they were drawing so much blood that it became so painful that I cried when they did it. I had to calm myself down for the children who were bringing patients candy for Halloween. I didn't want them to see me cry and possibly scare them. After days of eating just salad (you know how terrible hospital food is), I had one of the nurses tell me that they were trying to thin my blood and the salad wasn't helping. Once I stopped eating the salads, I was able to go home. Later I began my rounds of chemotherapy.

A Close Call

On Christmas Eve I wasn't feeling well and went to the doctor at Annapolis Naval Station. They said I had a sinus infection. On the way home I felt chilled to the bone. On Christmas morning I woke up with chills. I told Dee to ask my mom for some hot tea. She gave me tea with lemon in it. I drank it and threw up. I didn't feel any better. My mom tried to call the doctor, to no avail. She asked me, "Do you want me to take you to Bethesda?" I said, "No. I don't think I will make it there." I told her to call an ambulance. She and my dad carried me downstairs.

The ambulance arrived and wanted to take me to Provident Hospital because no more ambulances could come to Sinai Hospital because they had no room. My mom told them no. The EMT told her that they could help her get me into the car. My mom could drive me up to the door and they would have to take me. By the time I got there, I couldn't sit up. They had to bring a wheelchair to the car to get me in. My blood was drawn. A nurse came in and said, "Ms. Campbell, do you know you have no white blood cells in your body?" The next thing I knew they were taking me upstairs. In the meantime, my mother was still trying to reach my doctor.

My brother Alex came to see me. He said, "You better not go anywhere." I said, "I'm not." I started shivering. He gave me his fluffy Christmas hat. I smiled because he knew I loved it. Alex asked the nurse for extra blankets. Quite some time had gone by with no one coming with the blankets. He asked for them again. Still, no one came. By then the entire bed was shaking too. All I heard was him cussing in the hall.

Suddenly all these people came rushing into the room. I remember feeling like I was spinning in bed. I was being taken to Intensive Care. I was semi-conscious when I heard a male nurse say, "If she pulls through this, it will be a miracle." My only thought was that I couldn't do that to my mother. She lost her best friend to cancer two years prior on Christmas Day. A miracle happened; I survived. When I came to later, a nurse told me I was so hot that those around me were sweating. There were two blankets on me with cold water running through them. I passed out again.

When I came to the next day my mom and sister Yvette were in my room. Yvette said, "That doesn't even look like her." I passed out again. I woke up the next day and was moved to a regular room. My doctor called me to ask what happened. I told him. He said my mom was very angry and yelled at him. They had the wrong on-call doctor, that's why she couldn't reach him. He said I would be transferred to

A Close Call

NNMC. The doctor came in to tell me that my doctor from NNMC wanted me to be transferred there. I went into the bathroom when I could get up and saw my face in the mirror. I was shocked because I didn't recognize myself. My face was swollen and there were lots of little red spots all over my face and in my eyes. Blood vessels had burst from me throwing up. Another doctor I didn't recognize came into my room to tell me I was being transferred and then just sat in the chair not saying another word for an hour. He made a charge for it, but I explained what he had done. He billed the government as if he were one of my doctors.

Before I left Sinai, I noticed that my eyes were bulging, and I had a twitch in my head. My tongue was somewhat swollen. The ambulance attendants laughed at me. I found out later it was from an anti-nausea medicine that I had been given too much of.

Then it was discovered that the catheter in my chest had developed bacteria. The bacterium was treated and another one grew. That one was treated and then another one came back. After a couple of weeks of bacteria tag, going back and forth, the doctors decided to take the catheter out and put one in my groin so that I could continue chemotherapy. That was done at my bedside. Let me tell you, that was one of the most painful things that was done to me. The needle was thick in order for them to put the tubing in. The doctor stuck the needle in me several times before he was successful. He had never done this procedure before, so I was his guinea pig. I screamed so much that the lady in the bed next to me wanted to tell them to stop. After being there for so many days I started to get depressed. Four women had been put in my room and discharged while I stayed. One was in a coma. When she woke up, they sent her home and there I stayed. I spent New Year's alone in my room. It was seventy degrees outside, and I couldn't feel it. Depression set in.

Finally, the doctor said I could go home for one night. I came back the next day and he said I could go home for a few days. He didn't want me to get sick again. I went down to the Officer of the Day to tell him. He told me no, I couldn't leave. Dee and Diona were crushed. Dee cried. Diona had never had a tantrum before, but she lay on the floor crying. My dad had to pick her up and carry her out kicking and screaming. I cried. It really hurt seeing them like that. I told the doctor what happened, and he said I could go but had to be back on Friday morning to have a different type of catheter placed. I thought my mom and dad were probably not out of the garage yet. I ran so fast through the hospital. When I got outside, they were just driving out. I told my mom what happened. Diona and Dee were elated. I came back on Friday for my catheter placement. After I was discharged, I continued chemotherapy for another six months.

Chemotherapy

My mom and dad took turns taking me in for my treatments. If they could not, I would drive there, and they would come to get me. One of them would drive my car back. During one of my visits with the doctor, he told me not to go home and sit around feeling sorry for myself. He said he'd lost a lot of elderly patients because they did that. The nurses and staff were wonderful. So, Diona and I window shopped at Walmart every day and I began helping Renee with girl scouts.

I had to have a bone marrow biopsy, which was done in the office. I was given a pill that was supposed to relax me, but it didn't work. I screamed and cried through the procedure. When I came out, the receptionist said, "Somebody back there was screaming so loud patients were walking out." I said, "It was me." My doctor found out the next day and was furious. He said that they should not have allowed me to go through that much pain. If I needed another one, I would go into the OR.

Every year my family would spend a few days in Atlantic City over the Easter holiday. One night I sat at a slot machine listening to my gospel music, not paying attention. I heard the bells go off and started looking around to see who had won. I got excited when I realized it was me. The lady beside me told me that I could go and look for my friend and she would watch my machine. I told her that I would wait. I won $2500. I was elated but it soon turned to dread. I thought, I've never won anything. Does that mean I'm going to die? I got over that quickly. I went to my mom and dad's room and woke them up to tell them about my winnings. I gave them $500. The next day we went to a different casino. I played on two different machines. I won $200 on one and $300 on the other. I came home and my car broke down. The repairs cost me all the money I had won, only to find out I just needed to buy another car. Yvette said, "You should write a book."

God waited.

I thought my hair would fall out, but it never did. Only the permed hair broke off the new growth. After chemotherapy ended, I still suffered from back pain. I was put on Morphine, Percocet, and Elavil. I could not work. I was put on medical leave. I was told to file for a medical board. One doctor wanted me to be sent back to work because I had been on medical leave for several months. He even began yelling at me in his office when I asked to have paperwork done giving me more time off. I yelled back. His boss called him into his office and asked him why he was yelling at me, then told him to give me the paper. I did not work for a year. I eventually went back to work but only for a year.

My Dad's Last Year

In 1997, I was placed on the Temporary Disability Retired List. While I was at home, I spent a lot of time with my dad. That year he got sick. He had to be put on oxygen but refused to walk around with one of those little tanks. He struggled to get up the stairs. His knees and elbows swelled. Someone suggested giving him cherry juice. Cecelia picked up some from a natural food store. I gave my dad a cup that day and that night he ran up the stairs. I would sit at home to keep him company and give him whatever he needed. He finally told me I didn't have to stay with him all the time, so I would sometimes go and volunteer in Diona's kindergarten class.

At the end of June the following year, Diona graduated from kindergarten. We took the girl scouts camping. If I had known that it would be the last weekend with my dad… Renee took my dad to the doctor on Monday and later that day he passed out at the front door in our house. I was terrified trying to help him get up. He then got up as if nothing happened. I called his doctor and was told to keep an eye on him and if it happened again to take him to the hospital. The next day the doctor called and said his glucose level was high and he needed to be brought in. He said my dad would be admitted. I took him in. The nurse checked his glucose level and said, "The monitor says 500+; what does that mean?" Another nurse said, "It means his sugar is above 500." The nurse asked my dad where his shunt was. I got angry. I had to keep telling her that he didn't have one; he was not diabetic and was not on medication for it.

They did nothing for seven hours. A doctor finally saw him and requested that an IV be put in his arm. We waited two hours. When someone finally arrived from the IV team, she stated that the doctor didn't say "Stat". They gave him two bags of fluid and some insulin, still questioning him about not taking his medicine. I had to keep telling them, once again, that he wasn't on medication or dialysis.

Less than 48 hours later, my dad had a stroke. He kept telling me and my mom that he was going home. I thought he meant to the house. I kept telling him that he had to get better first. He said that every day until he couldn't talk anymore, and his eyes stayed closed. We were told by a nurse that he had a pool of blood in his head, so Alex and I rushed to the hospital. We couldn't get a doctor to come and talk to us. We stayed for a few hours. After we left, I prayed to God, asking him to make my dad well but if it was time for my dad to go then it was OK. They called in the middle of the night to say he had passed.

My mom wouldn't sue the hospital because she didn't want to relive his death. I always wondered if there was something else I could have done. When I saw his sister, she looked at the expression on my face and said, "There was nothing you could have done. You did everything right." I felt somewhat of a sense of relief. Later, I had a dream that my dad came to me and said it was okay.

A week after his passing, I spoke to the man who delivered the oxygen and he told me that my dad said he was satisfied with his life, and he was ready. Our mail lady used to stand at the gate and talk with my dad. I saw her one day and asked her what happened to her. She said when she found out, it really hurt, so she asked for her route to be changed. She said he was so nice to her and most people wouldn't spend time talking to her. When I would sit outside, many people would stop and ask what happened to the man who used to stand here at the gate. I told them he passed away. They were sorry to hear that because they used to talk to him and said that he was a very nice man. They all seemed to be visibly upset and said he would be missed. Some of the people I had only seen walking by the house and did not know they knew my dad. I continued to stay with my mom.

Meeting My Husband

In July of 2001, I attended a birthday party for my best friend Bridgett's dad. The guy cooking on the grill was extremely nice to me. He kept watching me. When he finished cooking, I saw him sitting on the back porch talking to Bridgett's sister. He kept staring at me. I had never met her husband, so I assumed it was him. I got uncomfortable and told Bridgett I was going home. Later, in September, my mom and I went to an Oldies but Goodies dance at the church. Bridgett introduced me to her cousin. His name was Michael. It was the guy on the grill from the cookout. They sat across the table watching and talking about me. He asked her for my number. She gave it to him. Michael later asked me to dance. Neither one of us could really dance. A friend's nephew came over and moved Michael out of the way. Michael went to dance with someone else. I was in shock. He came back to talk to me later. When the party was over, Michael walked me to his uncle's house next to the church to get my children. He kissed me on the forehead. There were cheers from his cousins on the porch. He exclaimed, "I'm going home with her tonight." My mom quickly said, "Oh no you're not." Everyone laughed.

A week later, Bridgett came to my mom's house. She said her mother and Michael's mom kept asking each other if he had called me yet. Michael's mom said he had been tearing up the house trying to find my number. I asked Bridgett to call him. She did. Michael and I talked on the phone for seven hours. We talked for several hours every night over the next year, except when we were together. Two weeks after our initial conversation, he asked me to marry him. He told me that if we broke up and I decided to go on a date with whomever I was seeing, I might as well make reservations for three, because he would be there with us.

I went camping with our girl scout troop at Camp Conowingo one weekend. We were in an area where we had no phone signal, so I couldn't talk to Michael. I was advised by his aunt to never do that again. She said he walked around like he had lost his best friend.

Michael accepted my children as if they were his. Every weekend we spent together, the girls came with us. He called me one night while cleaning his mother's carpet and sang Stevie Wonder's "For Once in My Life." We discovered that our birthdays were two days apart. He was born two years later than me. Thinking back, we may have met as children. But neither one of us remembers meeting each other. Michael tells people to this day that I thought I was too bougee and ignored him, although we both know that it's not true.

Meeting My Husband

During our courtship, I found out I had cardiomyopathy and a restrictive lung disease caused by chemotherapy and cancer. In April of 2002, Michael officially proposed to me in a restaurant. I thought he was joking and laughed at him. He was serious and I said yes. A few weeks later I found out I was pre-menopausal. We figured I didn't have much time if he wanted a child, so I became pregnant, much to the doctor's surprise. In July of 2002, we were both lying on the floor at my mom's house (he likes to sleep on the floor. He does it at all of our family's houses). I suddenly felt fluid running out of me. I called the VA hospital and spoke to my GYN nurse. She told me to go to the nearest hospital, which was five minutes away from me, only to find out later that she and the doctors from University of Maryland Medical Center were waiting for me at the VA Hospital. We went to the hospital around the corner. They did an ultrasound and said they didn't know where the fluid was coming from and that the baby was okay. We were so relieved. They told me that I could stand for no more than 15 minutes. At that time, I was working as a cashier at the commissary on the military base. When I went to work to let them know what the doctor said and showed them the papers, I was told that I either had to quit or be fired. So I quit. I decided that I was not going to put my baby's life in danger for that job.

The doctors placed me in an at-risk clinic. I had to have weekly ultrasounds and an amniocentesis to make sure that the baby was okay. We didn't ask them to tell us what the sex of the baby was. Michael said he didn't care as long as the baby was healthy. When the doctor called us to give the results of the amnio, she asked if we wanted to know the sex of the baby. I said no. Michael said yes. So I gave in to his wishes. When she told us it was a boy, Michael was ecstatic. Dee and Diona decided to name the baby Michael Junior, MJ for short. Michael didn't want a junior and I wanted to continue with the D names and name him Dion, but naming him MJ grew on me.

Tremors

On the evening of February 15, 2003, we were all in the living room watching a movie and everyone had fallen asleep except me. I suddenly had a strong contraction and it felt like my water was about to break. I jumped up off the couch, sprained my thumb and I screamed to Diona to wake up Michael. We rushed to the hospital. My contractions were not that strong. We were there for a while. The doctors broke the amniotic sac. With every contraction MJ's heart rate became low. They later told me that my contractions were so strong that they were killing my baby. The doctor told me that if I had another contraction like that, they would do a C-section. As soon as they walked out of the room, I had a contraction that took MJ's heart rate down to 4 bpm. Again, I prayed for my baby's life. They rushed back and told me that they were taking me to the operating room. I began to cry because I didn't want a C-section. Michael was taken out to get into a gown. A little while later they handed me my beautiful, healthy baby boy. He had gray eyes. Michael and I could not understand why his eyes were gray. It took us months to figure out that his eyes were that color because of Michael's mom. He was born during one of the worst snowstorms in the state of Maryland. My nurse had to stay the entire week with me. She could not leave because of the snow.

MJ was born a little jaundiced but otherwise okay. He spent a week in the NICU to clear the jaundice up. I was allowed to stay at the hospital with him. I was up and down so much during his stay that my staples began to come out. After that week I was able to take my baby boy home.

The day after his birth I began having tremors. I kept telling my primary care doctor about these tremors. She told me that she would not send me to neurology because she had not seen them. She kept telling me to videotape them. I told her that I didn't have a camcorder. One day while waiting outside her office, I had tremors. They took me to the emergency room, and she tried to explain to them what I had told her. She didn't give the correct information. She tried to act as if she had addressed them before and knew everything. I had to tell them as best as I could what happened and that everything my primary care doctor told them was wrong. The doctors gave me medication to try to stop them, but it did not work. I had four episodes while I was in the emergency room. They sent me home with nothing.

The next time that I was scheduled to see my doctor I had another one outside her door. Again, they took me to the emergency room. This time the neurologist came to see me, but they did nothing. For two years I was being told that I was not having seizures. Everyone who was not a doctor told me that I was. While I was working in Shoppers as a cashier, a doctor told me that was what was wrong with me, and it was caused by my epidural. Yvette said, "You should write a book."

God waited.

I was finally sent to see a neurologist. The doctor comes in and says, "You're having seizures." I began to laugh. She got mad and told me that it was not funny and that there were people suffering from them. I said, "Yes, it is because you all have been telling me for the last two years that's not what I was going through. And now you tell me that it is." She said that the seizures were called pseudo-seizures and they were caused by lack of sleep, caffeine, and stress. As of today, I still have them. MJ is 20 years old. She put me on Amitriptyline. They tried several other meds but nothing has worked.

Kidney Issues and Breast Cancer

My doctor sent me to nephrology because she found blood in my urine and my legs kept swelling. I explained to her that there had been blood in my urine throughout my military career and up to this day. I told her that they kept sending me for testing and despite being told several times that I needed a biopsy, one was never done. At first the nephrologist thought one of the medications for my heart caused the swelling in my legs. So he changed it. I went back because the swelling wouldn't go away. The nephrologist tried to tell me that the issues with my kidneys were because I had an injury to my back. I told him I had never been hit in the back. He then told me it was because of my weight. So I said, "What was wrong with me when I weighed 150 pounds less than I weigh now and I had the blood in my urine?" He got upset and said, "I don't know," and walked out. When I saw him again, he put me on Prednisone to slow down the progression of kidney failure. Over the course of the next year, I gained 50 pounds. I could barely walk. I had to be pushed around in a wheelchair. I hated that.

One day at the end of a workday I was struggling to breathe. Michael came to pick me up. I was very short of breath. He took me to the VA hospital. While I was in the emergency room the doctor asked me if I had noticed that my abdomen was getting bigger. I told him yes. He told me it was because my body was filling up with fluid. He told me that my legs were full, up to the middle of my thighs. I was admitted to the hospital. They put me on Lasix to get rid of the fluid. I woke up in the middle of the night and I could barely move. It took all my strength to call the nurse's station to let them know. They came into my room and took my pressure. It was very, very low. They called for the doctor to come and see me. The doctor said that they had taken off too much fluid, so they had to give me some back.

While I was there, one doctor asked me who my primary care doctor was and then told me that because of my extensive medical issues I needed an MD as my primary care doctor and not a nurse practitioner. She also said that I needed to be seen by specialists, including a cardiologist and a neurologist. They finally decided that I needed a kidney biopsy. In 2009, my biopsy was done. The biopsy determined that I had a kidney issue that they normally saw in children called Minimal Change Disease. The nephrologist told me that they would keep me off dialysis as long as possible.

Kidney Issues and Breast Cancer

Later that year I had a breast exam. The doctor found a lump but said they would just monitor it. In January of 2010, I decided to go back to school and enrolled in an online college. It was very intense and took away from any free time that I had. In April, they redid the exam with an ultrasound and said that there were more lumps and I needed to be scheduled for a biopsy. During that time the cardiologist discovered that my heart was weakening.

One Friday, my neck began hurting and no matter what I did it wouldn't stop. I went to a weekend sleepover with our Girl Scouts at Renee's house. I slept in my sister's chair all night because of the pain. The next morning, I felt a tearing sensation in the middle of my chest near my throat. It felt like all my energy was draining from my body. I told my sister that something wasn't right. She yelled for someone to call 911. My mom came running down. She hugged me. I began to cry. I told her that I didn't want to die. Diona wanted to know what was going on. Renee told the girls to go into the basement.

The paramedics came and took me to the hospital. They did an x-ray to make sure I hadn't ruptured my aorta. It was fine. I breathed a sigh of relief. They then discovered that my heart was functioning at 30%. They said I needed a defibrillator. I told them about the pending biopsy. They said they couldn't put the defibrillator in until they found out if I had breast cancer. I stayed for four days. The cardiologist and the breast surgeon at the VA kept going back and forth about the two surgeries because if I did have breast cancer and needed radiation, they would have to take out the defibrillator if they placed it beforehand. The breast surgeon wanted me to be cleared by cardiology. This lasted about two months. The biopsy was done in August of 2010.

I had spoken to one of Michael's cousins about my biopsy and she told me how painful it was for her. I was terrified. I met a woman in the lobby who was also there for a biopsy. She asked if she could pray for me and another woman waiting with us. I could feel the fear leave my body.

While being prepped for the biopsy I was having a ball. I was laughing and talking to the doctors and nurses while they were putting these black wires in my breast to mark the spots. Once they numbed me up it didn't hurt at all. The doctor said he had never had a patient so happy while they were doing that. He said I was his favorite patient. I even walked almost a block from the University of Maryland Hospital, where they placed the wires into my chest, back to the VA hospital, where the biopsy would be performed.

I was admitted to the hospital a few weeks later for another issue. While there, I had a scheduled appointment with the breast surgeon for my biopsy results. Normally, with admissions your appointments are cancelled. Instead, she said the doctor would come to my room to see me. The receptionist said that she didn't know how long the doctor would be because she had to make her rounds. Thinking she would be awhile, Michael left to go to McDonald's. I knew that as soon

Kidney Issues and Breast Cancer

he left, she would come into the room. She came in and told me that they discovered two carcinomas (ductal and lobular) in my breast. She said that never in her career had she ever seen two carcinomas in every piece of tissue that they took. She also told me that this was not the aggressive type of breast cancer. She said that they could take the right breast and just watch it to see if it developed in the left one. I could not have a lumpectomy because there was too much tissue involved and it would leave me misshapen. She asked me what I wanted to do. I told her that I would talk to my husband and we would let her know. I called my sister Cecelia while Michael was gone. She told me that I would be okay. Michael came back and I told him what she said. We both cried. We decided that I would allow them to take both of my breasts instead of me going through the pain of the surgery twice. He said that he would rather have me lose them than him lose me. A few days later, I received calls from the four surgeons who were in the OR with me for the biopsy. Each of them gave me the results and asked what I wanted to do. I told them that we decided to have them take both. They asked me if I was sure and I said yes.

I was terrified of having the surgery because of my heart and lungs. My only thoughts after that were that I was going to die in surgery. So I planned a game night a few days before the surgery, which happened to be my birthday, with my best friend Bridgett, my mother-in-law, Michael's aunt and cousin, and my family. The next day was my anniversary. My sister Renee and a friend wanted to take me out to celebrate my birthday. I hadn't told anyone about my fear, not even my husband. They prayed for me that night. The burden of fear was lifted once again.

Two days later I went into surgery with a smile on my face. The nurses injected some dye into my breast and said it needed to be massaged in. Michael gladly took the job. A nurse walked in and was surprised. We explained that the other nurse told us to do it and she laughed. I knew that God would see me through. Yvette said, "You should write a book."

God waited.

I cried a lot afterwards because I felt less than a woman. I continued my studies. I asked my professors for a two-week leave of absence because of the pain from moving my arms. One said yes, the other never answered until the week before finals. He gave me a D. I complained to the dean to no avail. Every now and then I look back and wonder if I should have waited to see if it would spread to the left breast. I stayed in the house for a while because I didn't want to be seen. Bridgett coaxed me out one day.

After a year and a half, the VA offered me prosthetics. I have a few funny stories about those things. When I would take them off, I often caught my son, who was nine at the time, and then later my little grandson, just rubbing or squeezing them. They felt like stress balls. Once I was in the pool at a cookout in Renee's backyard and one decided that it wanted to experience floating on its own. It floated out of my bathing suit. I hadn't realized that it happened. I turned around and saw it. My nephew was near me so I grabbed it before he could see it. Once I got out of the pool, I shared the story with my family. We laughed the rest of the night. I bought a regular bra to wear and decided to put the prosthetics in it so I could go to a party. While sitting and talking to Dee, I looked down and noticed one of the straps had popped off. The prosthetic was lying down, just sticking out. I frantically whispered to Dee to look and fix it. She did so without anyone noticing. I went inside and told Bridgett what happened. She laughed hysterically. I got home later and was taking off my clothes when I noticed that one of them was missing. I couldn't figure out what happened to it. Michael went outside to look and found it on the steps. Luckily the children playing outside didn't notice.

Kidney Failure

In 2011, I began working for a veteran's organization helping veterans with their claims. Some of the veterans would tell me that they would stop feeling sorry for themselves because I had worse problems and they could not tell from looking and talking to me. In 2013, I finally got my defibrillator put in. Dee gave birth to my grandson, Aidan and Oreo, my Shih Tzu, came into my life. In May 2014, we flew to Arizona for my graduation for my Bachelor of Arts Business Degree. In June of 2014, I called my nephrology nurse and told her that I really wasn't feeling well. I told her that I could not stand without getting really dizzy and I couldn't go to work. She told me to go to the VA hospital emergency room and tell them that I needed dialysis immediately. I went and was admitted. They told me that I would be put on dialysis. A catheter was placed in my chest. I stayed in the hospital for almost two weeks. The dialysis made my body feel like it was on fire.

In September of that year, a graft (made from synthetic fabric) was placed in my arm. My arm swelled up and has only somewhat gone down since then. Over the next year-and-a-half I went to the doctor several times for them to go into the graft and widen it because it constantly narrowed in some spots.

On February 28, 2016, I went to dialysis as I usually did. The tech put the needle in, only to pull out a clot. He kept trying to adjust it and it still kept getting clotted. He informed the nurse. She told me I needed to go to the access center where they specialized in dealing with clotted dialysis accesses. She had to get permission from the VA hospital first. I was told to go home until I was given further instructions. On the way out I began to cry. One of the technicians told me it would be okay, and it was something that happened. I hated going to the hospital because they liked to keep me.

Michael came and took me home and went back to work. I got a call later in the afternoon from the nurse saying the VA gave permission. Michael left work to take me to the access center. I was lying on the table when I heard the doctor say to the nurse, "Look at this. As soon as I clear the clot it comes right back. And now they're developing around her defibrillator wires. She needs to go to the hospital." To me she said, "Who is with you?" I said, "My husband." After stitching me back up, the doctor took me to the waiting room and told Michael he needed to take me to the hospital. She said, "Do not go home or anywhere else. Take her straight to the VA hospital."

Off we went. They were waiting for me when I arrived. I was placed on Heparin. The doctors debated about going in but decided not to. My arm swelled up so badly that I could not bend it or make a fist. They had to string it up to keep it elevated. Another catheter was placed in my chest so I could continue my dialysis. I was sent over to the University of Maryland next door for dialysis. During one session the tech never used any alcohol pads to clean my tubing, nor did he put on gloves. By the next morning, my pressure rose really high. I was told I was being moved to the ICU. I called Michael because I was scared. Suddenly I felt nauseous. I began throwing up. A nurse walking by came in. She panicked trying to hold me up and called for help. A doctor came in and I told her that I felt as if everything was draining out of me.

She said, "You're okay."

I said "You don't understand. I feel like all my energy is leaving my body."

They called for Rapid Response. The next thing I knew there were ten doctors and a pastor in my room. The pastor was standing by my head. I looked at him and said to myself, This is not happening today. They were going to use the lift to transfer me to a stretcher but there wasn't enough time. Instead, they said, "We need to hurry. We're taking her in the bed."

They moved me to the ICU. I was in and out of consciousness for 24 hours. While in and out, I kept seeing an image of God's face as if it were placed on one of those 3D pin art canvases. The background changed but the face remained. He kept telling me, "DON'T STRESS OUT. EVERYTHING WILL BE OKAY."

When I finally came to the next day, a woman walked into my room and asked if I wanted a Guidepost booklet. I said yes. She handed it to me. On the front it read DON'T BE STRESSED. I was floored. I told Michael that I would not complain about being there and wanting to go home. I would allow the doctors to do what they needed to do. I didn't want to rush and go home, only to have to come right back.

After being there for thirty-five days I was completely well, so I went home for two weeks. I then went back to the hospital because I was having pains in my chest. They told me that it wasn't my heart and that I was fine but my blood was too thin, so I had to stay. I stayed in the hospital for two weeks. A week later I was given some medication for a pinched nerve in my jaw. It caused me to have seizures. I went to the hospital and was admitted. I had shaken for four days. I stayed for ten. Finally, I went home for a while. During those hospital stays, whenever they would tell me I could go home, my stay was prolonged because my blood was either too thick or too thin. Yvette said, "You should write a book."

God waited.

One day at dialysis they checked to see if the clot was still there, and it had cleared up. The nurse was in shock. She called out to the staff to tell them that my clot had gone away. UNTIL…

January of 2017, I went in for dialysis and discovered that there was another clot in the graft. I was sent to the hospital. I was kept. They put another catheter in my chest. That catheter wouldn't stop bleeding. A technician from Interventional Radiology was sent to my room to stop the bleeding. We thought it stopped but it didn't. The doctor told them to bring me down for a replacement. They placed another one in my chest. That one began bleeding that night. The nurses placed padding around it. It bled through the padding. They ended up having to put the padding around to my back because the blood kept running. Because the clinic was closed, it just bled through the night. The doctor from the clinic came to my room the next day and he said, "Oh, that's not so bad." Then he got down to the bottom layer of the padding and said, "Oh my God, that's a lot of blood!" He put this purple gooey stuff on the incision. That stopped the bleeding.

Hysterectomy

During the five years prior, I was having a lot of vaginal bleeding. They told me I had uterine fibroids. The doctors tried everything: birth control, uterine fibroid embolization, and a dilation and curettage (D&C). The cardiologist had to turn off my defibrillator for the procedure. But he didn't do something right and I felt funny. It felt like my heart was beating in my throat. I told the nurse. She told me that there was nothing wrong. I kept telling her that I'd had them turn it off many times before and I never felt that way. The anesthesiologist asked me what was wrong. I explained to him what was wrong. By then he was yelling. He leaned down to me and told me not to worry because he would make sure nothing happened to me. He asked the nurses who was responsible for me, and no one answered. He said he would care for me as of that moment and told them to call the cardiologist. The head of cardiology came down with the doctor and told him that he skipped a step, causing me to have an extra heartbeat. The anesthesiologist later told me that had he put me under I would have died.

God Waited for Me

In October of 2018 my husband and I drove across the country to Las Vegas. We stopped in every state buying shot glasses, lottery tickets, and magnets. I won twelve dollars in Kansas. I think that everyone should drive or ride cross country at least once in their lives. It was beautiful, especially Utah. A few days after we returned, I went into the hospital for a hysterectomy because I continued to bleed on and off every week for years. They prepared me for surgery. I was finally ready to go into the OR. The anesthesiologist came in and said, "I'm sorry, we cannot do your surgery today. You must be cleared by the cardiologist." I was upset because we had been there for hours. I had mentally prepared myself to do this. I was told that once they got the clearance I would be rescheduled. I came back a month later. Again, I was ready to go into the OR. The surgeon said, "We are missing the cardiologist's signature." I said, "Are you kidding me? I was told that once they got it, I would then be scheduled." The surgeon said to the nurse, "We are doing this today. Run across the bridge and get the signature." We waited for 30 minutes. The nurse came back with the papers signed, and I went in for surgery.

Dialysis Grafts, Catheters, and Fistulas

On December 4, 2018, I was lying in my bed. I suddenly felt as if I was going to pass out. This sensation was normal except this time it wouldn't go away. I asked Michael to take my pressure. It was low. We continued to take it for about twenty-five minutes. It remained low. Michael said, "Come on, Dawn. Let's go."

We drove to the VA hospital. Of course, when I got there my pressure was normal. They took me back to a room and after I was hooked up to a monitor my pressure went down again. So they drew blood. They told me I was dehydrated. I was given IV fluids and it would not come up. Later I was moved up to MICU. I was given more fluid. My pressure remained low and kept dropping. I was given more fluid.

The doctors constantly dropped by. I questioned them about the amount of fluid they were giving me because I didn't want to be overloaded. They explained to me that they thought my low pressure was due to an excess amount of fluid being removed at my dialysis session. I was sent for an ultrasound and a CT scan of my heart and lungs. They also ran more blood tests. My blood pressure began to rise. I was informed that my dry weight needed to be changed from 107.5 kg to 112.5 kg. I was very disappointed. That meant that I had gained weight. I tried to stop them. They informed me that the test that shows them the amount of fluid in a person's blood when on dialysis is usually abnormal. When the test was run on me after they gave me the fluid mine was normal. One doctor said, "We have never seen that in a dialysis patient." On Friday, I was given dialysis without the removal of fluid. They told me that they weren't sure how long I would be there. A couple of hours later I was sent home.

I went to the hospital and had the first part of the surgery for a fistula, where they connect a vein to the artery. I was told that I would need a second surgery to bring that vein up to the surface for dialysis access. After six months I had an ultrasound that showed narrowing of the vein. Surgery was scheduled to see if the vein could be opened. The doctor informed me that if the vein could not be opened then he would put in a graft. He told me that he tried several times to stretch the vein open and it immediately narrowed. So, he put a graft in my arm.

On May 2, 2019, I went to dialysis as usual. The two needles were placed. The machine was turned on. The alarms went off. My arterial pressure was high. After several adjustments

Dialysis Grafts, Catheters, and Fistulas

it began to hurt. The tech asked if I wanted another needle. I said yes. Another needle was placed. The same thing happened. A second needle was placed in the venous line. The high pressure continued. I was taken off the machine and awaited a response from the VA concerning what to do. After a few hours I was told to go to the VA's emergency room. I was told that part of the graft was narrowing. The doctor had to do an angioplasty to open it. It was okay for a few months. November came and it had to be done again. I went to dialysis the following day and the graft was clotted. A couple of days later I had to go in and have a catheter placed in my right thigh.

In May of 2020, the previous catheter was taken out and one was placed in my left thigh because the doctors decided that they were going to put a fistula in my right thigh. The surgery was completed after eight weeks of healing. The complication was that my leg would not stop swelling so they had to keep it wrapped in an Ace bandage. They also inserted a drain to keep the fluid from building in my leg, there was blood continuously in the drain and they could not figure out where it was coming from. The pain was excruciating. I asked them how they cut me, as they had told me that there would only be two small incisions. I found out that they cut me from my groin to my knee. They used staples to close the incision. Blood continued to drain. The doctors did not give me my warfarin to see if that would take care of the issue. Nothing went smoothly at this point. My pressure kept dropping and they were not sure if the readings were accurate, but they gave me something to increase the pressure. I had to have an arterial catheter placed in my arm. More pain. The pressures were at most times still not reading well. They noticed that at one point they were not reading at all. They had to have a doctor come in to exchange the catheter. I was anxious because I was fearful that it might hurt. The doctor informed me that it would not. My nurse stood beside me and held my hand. It didn't hurt at all. I stayed in the hospital for two weeks.

When I came home, I could barely walk. After taking thirty minutes for Michael and MJ to get me up the sidewalk, I tried to go up the five stairs to get into the house. My leg gave out on me. I fell in the doorway. I sat there for twenty minutes. I couldn't get up. Fluid was draining out of my leg. Dee and Michael got me up when I felt like I could do it.

I bought a chair to sleep in—bad idea. My plan was to sleep downstairs. The chair was uncomfortable, so I put a pillow on the seat. I moved around on the seat and slid off it onto the floor. Michael had gone to the store. He walked in and asked me how I got down there. Michael, Dee, and MJ got me up. I told them that this wasn't going to work and I wanted to go upstairs. It took two hours to get me up there. Every day that I had to go to dialysis was a family effort to get me in and out of the house.

Travel

Michael and I love to travel. I love to drive. Our first adventure was to Myrtle Beach, South Carolina, where we spent our honeymoon. For our 10th anniversary, we rented a cabin in Virginia. My daughter talked about all the horror movies with cabins in the woods, which made me very nervous. The cabin had only one bathroom that was downstairs. I had to go to the bathroom in the middle of the night. Michael wouldn't come with me. I crouched down low to avoid the windows. I didn't want to look out of them in fear that I would see someone looking back at me. We went to Shenandoah National Park to do an informal renewing of our vows and take pictures in our wedding attire. We drew a lot of attention, trying to find the perfect lookout spot for our photo. A ranger volunteered to be our photographer. Funny story, Michael thought it was okay to really get back to nature while we were in the woods. He stepped out onto the deck in his birthday suit. I called his mom because he refused to come inside when I asked him. She laughed. The deer thought he was crazy. The next morning while cooking breakfast, Michael yelled to me that a deer was at the window staring at him. After this, we decided we would go away every year for our birthdays/anniversary. Next up, Pigeon Forge, Tennessee. We drove up into the Great Smokey Mountains hoping to see wildlife but saw none. The exciting thing was that at the top, you are in Tennessee and North Carolina at the same time. Michael has acrophobia (fear of heights). Driving up into the mountains terrifies him. He did drive up some of the way. That was my first experience of standing above a cloud. In town, we went to take photos at an Olde Tyme studio. Michael was a gangster. He looked so handsome in a hat.

I was so excited to see the Dollywood sign just so that I could take a picture. So, we followed the signs and drove into the parking lot to get a picture. Much to my surprise, you can't see the sign because it is blocked by trees. You can't even see any of the park. I will go back one day just to go in and try the awesome food that I have seen on television.

Our next cabin rental was in Blue Ridge, Georgia. It was called "The Cloud Lodge". The view was amazing. I woke up one morning to fog at the patio doors. It reminded me of the movie "The Fog". It was kind of creepy. While it was receding, it looked like waves. It was so beautiful. I would wake up in the morning to record the sunrises. Michael and I got to watch a meteor shower in the middle of the night. There were even turkeys wandering on the road at night. An apple orchard was down the road from us. We discovered fried fruit

Travel

pies there. They were delicious. I found out how they make pork rinds. They take pork skins and deep fry them. We loved the fruit pies and pork rinds so much that we went back on the morning that we were going home to get some to take with us. In the opposite direction, we shared a long-distance love. Each of us stood on the opposite sides of the yellow line down the road that indicated the state line between Georgia and Tennessee. When we got home, Oreo decided that he would eat one of the bags of pork rinds under my bed.

Our second trip to Las Vegas was harrowing. Once we got into the Rocky Mountains in Colorado, we found out that there was a mudslide that trapped one hundred people. They rerouted us. Instead of following their directions, we used the car's GPS. Well, it took us into the middle of nowhere. We got tired and had to search to find a hotel for the night. We got the last room at a Holiday Inn. The next day was horrible. The reroute took us on a two-lane road. The road had no guardrail. I was driving on a cliff. I white-knuckled it. I prayed and asked God to hold my hands steady. One wrong move and over the cliff we would go. On the way down, I was creeping but this time I was near a rock wall. At a curve, there was a large rock formation jutting out into the road. The lane narrowed so much that it was smaller than the width of my car, then there was no line in the middle of the road. As I was coming around the blind curve, an SUV came flying around the curve in the middle of the road. Luckily, I was moving slowly because I was able to stop as soon as I saw him. I'm quite sure that the people behind me were relieved. If an accident had happened, we would have been stuck for hours as there was traffic in both directions.

I won't bore you with all the details of our other trips but I will tell you that we have been to Virginia Beach, Virginia where I sat on a balcony recording a lightning show, Wildwood, New Jersey, back to Pigeon Forge with my mom, Yvette, and Renee and Stamford, Connecticut, where we saw a movie and got popcorn and drinks for less than twenty dollars. So, as you can see, I don't let any of my illnesses hold me back.

God Answers

The evening of February 21, 2021, I felt a little dizzy, so I asked Michael to help me go to the bathroom. When I was done, I asked him to help me go back to the bedroom. I told him I didn't feel well, so we leaned against the wall. I said I needed to sit down. I asked him if he needed help from MJ. He told me that he had it. So we took a couple of steps into the hallway. I started falling, he grabbed me, and we both went to the floor. MJ came running. MJ said, "How did you both end up down there?" Dee came running up the stairs and said, "Oh my God." They helped Michael get me up and to bed. Maybe half an hour later I decided I wanted some ice cream but before that I drank some lemonade. As you know, lemonade and ice cream don't mix. My stomach began churning. I had to go to the bathroom again. I managed to get up and go to the bathroom, but I got dizzy again. I called Michael and MJ to help me get back to bed.

About 2:30 in the morning, I called Michael to tell him that I was about to fall out of bed. I had to call him twice because he was sleeping. By the time he got to the other side, I was on the floor. I got that feeling that my pressure had dropped. He took my pressure. It was low. He took it once more and it had gone up. It just kept going up and down. I told Michael that I would go to dialysis. I changed my mind because I told him that they would send me to the hospital. I said I would go to the VA instead. Michael and MJ took me to the car.

By the time I got to the hospital I was dizzy. My eyes were moving back and forth, and I was having a seizure. The doctors couldn't figure out what was going on because there were so many things happening at once. They thought that maybe there was too much fluid taken off me but giving me fluid didn't help the situation. The doctors requested a culture of my blood. Blood was drawn from the arterial side of my catheter. The neurologist was called in. He was amazed that my eyes were going back and forth like they were and that I was shaking. One of the doctors was examining me. I said, "Uh-oh, here it comes again." I began having another seizure. He was shocked. I kept telling Michael I was scared. He tried to comfort me. Doctor after doctor came into my room. I was told I would be admitted. A little while later, I was moved to the floor. I was taken to dialysis, as this was my scheduled day. The nurse said she couldn't give it to me because my pressure was too low, so I was taken back to my room. While I was there, neurology came back to examine me again. They discussed my eyes moving back and forth and the jerking movements of my hands. I continued to have seizures.

Later my pressure dropped so low that many doctors ended up in my room. They told me I was being moved to the ICU to be closely monitored. While in ICU I was given a 24-hour dialysis. I told the doctor that I was having pelvic pain. She just said OK. Doctors kept coming in, telling me that I had an infection in my catheter and that it needed to be exchanged. I told them that I didn't believe that was what was happening. I explained to them that I only had one more area where the catheter could be placed. I had been told by the Interventional Radiologist that he didn't want to keep messing with it because this was the next to the last resort. We continued to disagree for a few days. I asked God for guidance and a sign.

The next morning, I was told that I was stable enough to be moved downstairs to a regular room. Later, a doctor came into my room to talk to me. She said she was going to be taking care of me once I was moved downstairs. She spoke to me about getting the catheter exchanged, asking me if I knew what sepsis was. After I told her yes, she decided to explain anyway. Because I knew this was the sign, I told her that I would not argue anymore and would allow them to exchange the line. I was moved to the third floor.

Once I was in my room, the students from the medical team came in. They told me the name of the doctor who was heading the team. I said that I had met her. I waited for her to come in. It was not the doctor I met in the ICU who was supposed to be taking care of me. I was in shock. I never saw the doctor from the ICU again. They both had the same name. The sign: God needed someone to convince me of the seriousness of what was possibly happening to me. The new doctor began explaining the dialysis process to me. I told her I had been on dialysis for seven years and I knew how the process worked. She continued to explain because she had to get to another point. I allowed the doctor to speak.

That night I had severe pain in my pelvis. The doctor was called, and I was given pain medicine. The next morning the pain was back but with more intensity. They sent me down for a CT scan. I found out that the pain in my pelvis was from bleeding in the deep muscles in both sides of my back. I had been complaining about this for a year. My primary care doctor told me that it was arthritis.

I got a call from the endocrinologist telling me that my adrenal gland might have been causing my pressure to be low so they would do a blood test to see. The blood test revealed that my adrenal gland was fine and not the reason. They wanted me to decide whether to go back on the blood thinner. I asked God to help me. I received another sign. My blood clotted in the chamber at the end of my dialysis. I was finally discharged on Thursday, after staying for two and a half weeks. Yvette said, "You should write a book." I told her that I thought that God was using her as a messenger to tell me what my purpose was.

And still He waited.

Panic Attacks

On Tuesday of the following week, after picking up Michael, I stopped at the gas station. My muscles started cramping. I ignored it because I thought it was just a seizure. It took a while for me to regain movement, which is normal. When it ended Michael took me to the other side of the car. I asked him to take me to the store. He couldn't believe it. When we came out of the store, Michael asked me if I wanted to drive. I said yes. I noticed the stiffness in my leg again. Once we were home, my stiffness continued as I walked into the house. Later I received a call. While I was talking, I noticed my muscles throughout my body were cramping. I fought it and continued talking. Afterwards, I told Michael and decided to just go to sleep, hoping it would just go away and I would be fine in the morning.

I slept until the alarm went off. When I woke up, I had a creepy feeling go through my body. I told Michael we had to go back to the hospital. I could speak but no one except Michael could understand me. They allowed him to go in the back with me. By the time Michael got me on the gurney, I couldn't move at all. When the doctor came in, he removed my mask and his to understand what I was saying. He still had to ask Michael what I said. They sent in an intern. I explained to him that I suffered from seizures. I told him I felt one coming on. He seemed to be shocked when it started. It didn't last long. I went back to not being able to move again.

Motion returned sporadically in my arms and legs. During one of those moments, I asked Michael to play one of the mindful meditations tracks I liked to listen to. I cramped up again. I asked him to play my favorite gospel song. He played it. I began to move again. He told me what the next song was, and I just asked for my phone. I played more songs and prayed. I began to move my entire body. I never cramped again while I was there. The doctors said it was caused by one of my medications.

I was discharged on Thursday. On Friday, my husband and I were supposed to go for a weekend away to Charles Town Casino. But instead, after dialysis, I had a weird feeling in my throat. I continued with my day, taking my son to the phone store and getting something to eat. During that time, I kept having a little chest pain. Afterward, we picked my husband up and went home. The pain continued. My heart was racing to the point of feeling it in my throat. I took my medication to stop it and went to sleep. I woke up an hour and a half later and it was still there. I sat up, hoping it would get better. It didn't. I sat up further. No luck. I sat on the side of the bed

Panic Attacks

for a while. Still going. So I told Michael that I needed to go to the hospital.

They kept me for three days. There was nothing wrong with my heart. I was discharged on Sunday. A few days later I was back in the ER. They ran the same tests—again, nothing wrong with my heart. The pounding continued. The lights were turned down in my room in hopes that would make it better. Dread came over me. I began feeling like this was the end of my life. I called the doctor. In tears, I begged her not to leave me alone. She checked my pressure. It was high. She told me I needed to calm down and get some rest. I took some slow breaths and fell asleep. She came in later and told me I was having a panic attack. She sent me home.

I spoke to my sister Yvette the next day. She prayed for me. Afterwards, I felt like a weight had been lifted from me. I felt like I could float. I had not been this happy in a long time. This happiness was different. We talked for a few hours. After we hung up, I called everyone to tell them about my feelings. She joined our family prayer that night and prayed for my family.

Not long after this, my kidney doctor suggested that a transplant workup be done on me. She said I could only have one if I had a living donor. Renee, Willie, and Alex volunteered. Willie was taken off the list immediately because he smoked. Renee and Alex wouldn't be tested until I was cleared. The process began: an echocardiogram, a chest x-ray, psychological screening, and many blood tests. After that I had to get approval. I waited and waited for the results. I was on the phone with my mom when a call came on the other line. It was the transplant social worker. She told me that the doctors said I couldn't get a transplant. My heart and lungs were not strong enough. My heart dropped for a minute. I clicked back over to my mom. I told her what they said. She said, "It will be all right." I said, "I know. God knew it was not safe for me, so he told the doctors not to do it. I'm fine with that." I told my family. They were upset at first. Renee, Yvette, and my BFF Bridgett all repeated, word for word, what I had said to my mom. I told Michael. He cried. I told him that it was okay; God would take care of me.

COVID

Fast forward to October 2021: My family decided that we were going to get together for Christmas this year. So began the argument of who had been vaccinated and who had not, which then began the argument of who was not coming. It was decided that the unvaccinated would get tested prior to coming. We had a great time, although some of us were in masks.

A week later Diona came to my house when I was not home and spent some time with Dee and Aidan. On Monday, she called and said that she had COVID. Dee was the first to get sick. On Wednesday, I decided that my entire household would get tested. That night I began coughing a little. Thursday, I called the dialysis center to report my symptoms and asked them what to do. The nurse told me that she wasn't sure, and she would call me back. She never called.

On Friday, I left home to go to dialysis and called them before I got there. I was told not to come in. I asked what I was supposed to do and was told that they were not sure and would call me back. I never got a call. Later that night

Michael started coughing and throwing up. MJ's results came back negative. Dee was positive.

I waited until Saturday afternoon for the call from the dialysis center and still nothing. I went to the VA hospital because I needed dialysis. They tested me. I was positive. I was admitted. They put me in the ICU. Michael called me later and told me that he was positive too. I explained to the doctor that I had not had dialysis since Wednesday. She told me that they didn't have the staff to do the dialysis in the treatment center. She said that they would monitor my labs and if the results were high then they would give me dialysis. Aidan's and my results came back on Monday. I was positive and he was negative.

Tuesday, six days since my last dialysis, I woke up with a tingling sensation all over my body. I kept feeling like my body was telling me not to breathe. I called a nurse. She stood outside the door and told me that my oxygen saturation was fine. I told her how I felt, and another nurse told her to lean me back and give me oxygen. They called the doctor. She came in and told me that it was probably because the toxins were building in my body and that the dialysis tech was coming right in. I was mad because I didn't think that they should have let me go this long without it. They finally gave me dialysis. I was discharged the next day to go to the designated center to get dialysis again. I was upset with my home center because they didn't know what the protocol was for patients in my situation. I was over COVID before I went back to my center.

Dee was very sick. Michael had to take her to the hospital while I was still at the VA. They treated her in the waiting area, and she felt a lot better but retained some of the symptoms. Michael was sick for ten days. He developed the hiccups. He even did it in his sleep. Aidan had to stay in the room with MJ. MJ had to care for everyone.

In February, my back began to hurt. I started going to acupuncture in March for my jaw pain because it had returned with a vengeance. March came and went. My back was still hurting. I thought it was just a pulled muscle. After acupuncture ended in April, Michael and I decided to go away for a few days to spend some time together. My back just kept getting worse.

I was only home for a few days. I had to go to the emergency room five times through the course of my back hurting because the pain was so bad. I had to have help just to roll over in bed. X-rays and CT scans showed nothing. I was given different meds. The painkillers that worked could only be given to me in the emergency room. They even tried a pain patch that did not work. I woke up one morning with severe pain in my hip. MJ and Dee tried to move me while I screamed in agony. Michael came home so that MJ could take me to the hospital. It took two hours to get me out of the house.

They did another CT scan. Something showed up on my spine. They ran cultures and told me that I had an infection on my spine. I had no symptoms of an infection—no fever, no nausea, and no headache. They treated me with an antibiotic. It took a few days for them to figure out exactly what type of infection I had. I stayed in the hospital for two weeks. The doctors were fantastic. I was kept up to date with what they were planning to do. By the time I left the hospital the pain was not so bad. Don't get me wrong; it was still there but not to the extreme that it was.

October 2022, I was preparing to go to my niece's wedding, and I was overwhelmed because I had so much to do. I left for dialysis one morning and started having a panic attack. I said, "No, no, no." Michael asked, "What is wrong?"

I said, "I don't feel right." He told me to pull over somewhere so he could drive. The Cece Winans song "The Goodness of God" came on. I said, "Thank you, Lord" and the panic attack disappeared. I had another one later talking to Michael, while telling him that I was fine. I turned on another one of her songs called "I Believe For It" and that one also went away.

Death Came Calling

For some strange reason, in early December 2022, I was going in and out of dialysis at the same weight. Because of this there was no fluid being taken off me. I started feeling like I could not breathe. On Monday, I had the tech take off an extra 1.5kg but only 1.5kg was taken off. On that Wednesday, I had planned to have them take off 3kg. That did not work out. I was short of breath. They had to call an ambulance. While in the ambulance, I kept explaining to the EMT that I couldn't breathe, and she kept telling me that my saturation was fine. I told her that I felt that I was going to stop breathing. As soon as she put the oxygen mask on my face, I passed out. When I came to, there were several doctors around me saying that I didn't have pneumonia. They cut off one of my favorite dresses. They were going to cut my bra when they noticed that it unfastened in the front. I stayed in the ICU for a couple of days then was moved to a regular room the day before I was discharged. They took off thirteen pounds of fluid.

This section may not make sense, but I want you to understand the state that I was in the day after I returned home from the hospital. These are the exact words of my speech-to-text:

To end 2022 out, I went to the hospital yes I couldn't breathe When I got there no more I talked the more I got and then I told them that I was going out as I felt myself about to fall out trying to take my clothes off I said I was going out apparently I did And when I say I went out I actually died and it's a bag me I found out later and then they put they had to intubate me what I kept trying to pull the tube out of my mouth I kept trying to tell them that I need water it's all Michael They told MJ to call Michael because I was not responsive and MJ just thought that I was having a seizure that's what he told Michael I kept trying to fight because I wanted the tube out of my throat and I wanted some water so they had to sedate me what they do what they do what they do what they do when they do what in a hospital bit but the place that I was in everything was gold So I thought I was in a hospital and I didn't know that the VA had a place like that what suddenly I started going down and as I started going down I kept saying no no just can't be right can't be right And what I saw was everything that I hate it being around I hate it seeing and I just kept saying no it doesn't be right like I pray every day I've been bringing my family to you this can't be right and then I saw a student desk and a chair Sitting by a tree and I saw all of these roots so I went to sit down me the desk and chair to start it floating and I'll ask all those roots but I saw a light above my head and I just started floating up and I opened my eyes I saw I was at the hospital and the there was doctors around me But I still kept trying to get this thing out of my throat cause I wanted water so I heard Michael's voice say Dawn you need to calm down and do what they told you but I kept fighting and then he was gone The doctors kept telling me different things that they were going to do this was 2 days later the doctors kept telling me what they were gonna do and I'm saying OK but the scenarios of every time they came in my room Just kept playing over and over and over and over and over and over again so they told me they wanted to take The tube out of my mouth and I prayed and I say Lord if it's my time and it's your will and so be it I'm not afraid but I was upset after I closed my eyes and I just felt this sinking feeling and I kept apologized to my children and my husband So when it was trying to take the tube out I was fighting them but apparently I went out again and I saw my funeral but it wasn't like I thought it would be everybody was in black with If all these colors on a clothes it that was music it was kind of like a funeral in New Orleans I told the doctor asked him for something to write with told them I didn't want them to take the tube out because I saw my funeral I was at my funeral and and so They said Back later and try again so I said OK This scenario just played over and over and over again and there were like 4 of them that just kept playing and I was like Lord I feel like you're trying to tell me something but I don't know what it is and it has something to do with me dying and I said that if it's your will then it's your will I said Oh what's your still trying to tell me something that's why these scenarios are playing over and over again I said but the one where I saw my funeral was when they would try to take the tube well I said so when they tried to take this tube out I'm going to follow their instructions and let them pull it out so after they were when they came back to take it out I just followed the instructions and they pulled it out they told me that my lungs were clear And they kept having me swallow they say we're gonna do it A swallowing test and so they gave me some water and let me take a little small sips and then say but I talked to the doctor and I kept explaining to them about the scenarios repeating and repeating and repeating and she said but the one scenario that you didn't see was the one that went out we were trying to take the tube out That's the only one that didn't play over so I figured that was the only that I need to pay attention 2 so I made that decision to follow the instructions and everything was OK but so the thing I didn't say in the beginning was the reason that I couldn't breathe was my lungs where completely filled with fluid So they get me on 24 hour dialysis so they kept try to get rid of this Infection or whatever it was that I had but they were giving me so much medicine that they had to put an IV in my neck and because of that as you can see my neck is swollen and it's painful so whatever's and why it swelled up it's because there was blood leaking from my artery In my neck so right now there's a lot of blood in my neck and it won't go down until the blood is absorbed I didn't know that MJ was in the room when I died but he didn't understand what was two nurses that I've come to know over the years who were came in and first they were trying to put my hair together because they were like oh my goodness I am look so pretty and it was like no we got more pressing stuff to do Cause I needed to just stay what my hair all over the place but we need to save your life Over the course of those days different nurses and doctors kept coming into my room saying oh my God you look so good because that other day you was like it was terrible but we wouldn't gonna leave it do it everything in our power because we said we weren't gonna let you die Because of my neck I was in severe pain they had to do all of these CAT scans. Base to look at this thing on the side of my neck and to make check my chest and make sure everything was clear I had slept in from That time I woke up on Saturday morning until I think I slept maybe a hour on Monday night and then I didn't sleep again until after I got home but I don't think I slept that though but here's the weird thing is the panels on a ceiling at the yard they have all the little holes in it I saw all these different faces in the holes that is a hole but I kept looking at him and I saw faces I saw families I saw groups of people but I kept seeing these faces so the really weird thing was apparently I'd say the commercial did he have these black balls in it and they would like bouncing on a surface And then they started going into a hole like there's a game that's like that my problem was these balls turn into faces of people food some reason they had long hair no matter whether they were male or female so they turned into celebrities and the people that I know it was just weird and then after a while I got tired of seeing it on every time I close my eye I so I decided OK what about the kittens I wanna see the cat so did my eyes change to cat light but then the more I'm headed kept seeing it add capacity and ease the faces started turning evil and it was horrible and then they would just it could be 2 faces next to each other but they were next to each other they actually chill it the evil one would eat the other Added it to the point where I really didn't want to close my eyes but I kept trying to make it go away but it didn't and I kept telling that I told the doctor about it and he told me that this was happening because of everything that I went through and that it would go away after a few days so I also kept hearing the alarm sound From my phone but I guess it was the person next door I don't know how many times their phone went off but it was the same ring told that I had on my phone and I guess even when it wasn't going off I kept hearing it in my head over and over again for a few days and it was driving me crazy Bixby but I am I could only lay on my back With dialysis just constantly running the same way they took off they said 8 pounds of fluid from my alarms I I'm still not I'm never afraid about me dying because I don't have any control over it I also realized that That I need to I feel like I read a one of my verses that I read in the morning and evening and 1 of them talked about testing God and that's another thing that that came up into my mind is that no way that put too much potassium in your system can't kill you I've been still eating for a try as in everything Which is one of the foods that they tell us to watch me about intake and I just ate them saying oh I gotta die you know gotta go let me die but I can't do that so I need to follow the instructions and just take the medicine on Tuesdays and Thursdays it's and so that I am able to eat My potato stuffed tomatoes and tomatoes still feel like I'm leaving something out but I'm not sure what it was maybe it'll come to me of by the time I everything is to you guys but it was pain was horrible having it thing in my throat was horrible I want it out I can't try to tell the water But I found out that they made Michael leave the room because they thought that I was trying to get to him when I was trying to save water but of course we've just taken my throat I couldn't talk and I wanted it out so I could tell them what I was trying to say I'm quite sure that this is something that will be talked about every time I see anybody that was there when all of this happened well tab what I do thank God for those doctors and nurses that will it's the same alive cause I didn't pray and it's as God to only send those who invented you his will And he did and I'm still here so it's a talk about it but I knew that something that happened to me also because it was something that I asked them to do around the house and I don't even know what it was that came to tell me that it was done but I didn't talk to you 80 of our previous relatives that passed away I didn't see anybody because I never got To really anywhere close to the light but at all times I thought that I had actually died a bit of a while I've got that but this is that a Of message to say that I am a victim that I'm gonna die at each time no no stop what this is it's a story it's my testimony that God was with me in the entire time but he wanted me to figure out what it was that he just tried to tell me *and I did But some of the stuff I don't remember what happened other than me be in there so The Times that I was waking up trying to pull the thing on my throat I'll that's the only thing I remember I do you ever nurse this hole in my a** that try to keep me from pulling it out and tell it be that I needed to calm down and I needed to lay down It breaks my heart that MJ was there and I'm glad that he didn't really eat it I understand what was happening because I don't know what he would have done I'm having to go to get Michael and having to drive the car by himself knowing that I died But I'll be here to be with my family and I thank God then I love you all I said I wouldn't tell anybody this story until I told you I mean I told I told Dee and MJ at might go but I haven't showed the Diona yet because when I called her she was on her way to the house but I love you. As of now I still have pain in my feet, legs, chest, arms, and back. I deal with all of it because God has seen me through it all and I am still here.*

I had no idea that this was what was coming out of my mouth.

So that you can understand exactly what happened, I will explain. I was short of breath and decided to go to the store with MJ before going to the hospital. After coming out of the store, I felt like I was going to pass out. I started to tell MJ to call 911. It was raining outside. I decided I would go to the VA hospital instead. I didn't let MJ drive because I needed to get there in a hurry, and I didn't want him to drive fast in the rain.

We got to the hospital and I told them that I couldn't breathe. The more I talked, the harder it was to breathe.

Death Came Calling

When they took me back into a room, they wanted me to get on the gurney. I told them that I wanted to take my pants off first. I told the nurse that I was going out. I passed out. I stopped breathing. The nurse told MJ to call Michael because I was non-responsive. He called Michael. Michael asked MJ if I was having a seizure and MJ said he guessed I was. They had to bag me and then intubate me. I kept trying to pull the tube out. Michael came into my room and I kept trying to tell him that I wanted water, by signing the letters, hoping someone would understand me, that I was not trying to pull the tube out. They were restraining me. Michael kept holding my hands and telling me that I needed to calm down and do what the nurses told me. Then he was gone. The doctors had the nurses tie me to the bed. They had to sedate me. I was placed on 24-hour dialysis. I remember Michael coming to see me several times.

I was in and out for three days—at least, I thought I was. During that time, I kept hearing voices telling me that I was at the VA hospital and that I was safe. I remember looking up around and seeing that everything was gold and white. I thought to myself, *Wow, this place is beautiful. I didn't know the VA had a place like this. Is this the place where they put patients who are in hospice? Am I in hospice? Am I actually awake? I'm not sure.* The doctors would come in and wake me to explain what they were going to do. The scenarios of them coming into my room kept playing in my mind repeatedly. I remember Michael coming in to see me. It seemed like only for a few minutes. I'm not sure how long I was conscious. Every time the scenarios would play, I would ask the doctor if he had already told me that. I would feel my body and tell myself I was in a situation like in the movie *Groundhog Day*. I knew that some things should have changed but they would be the same way as they were when he told me. I thought I was losing my mind.

The respiratory nurse came in after I woke up to tell me that they would be taking the tube out later. I closed my eyes after she left, and I was at my funeral. Everyone was dressed in black clothing with lots of colors on it. A jazz band was playing like in New Orleans. We were on a pier near the water. They came into my room to take the tube from my throat. I told them no. They asked me why. I moved my hand, indicating to them that I wanted to write. I told them that I was at my funeral. I was in tears. They told me to calm down and that they would come back later.

The scenarios continued every time I closed my eyes. I asked God if He was trying to tell me that my life was over. I began to apologize to Michael and my children because I didn't know if my life was over. I told God that if it was my time then I wasn't afraid. Suddenly, I felt this sinking feeling like I was going through the bed. I began to go down, through the bed and through the ground. I saw everything that I hated. I said, "No God, this can't be right. I'm a good person. I pray every day. I brought my family to You." I looked to my right and saw a desk and chair sitting by a tree. There were big roots all around me. I went over to the desk and sat down. Suddenly the desk and chair began floating. There was a light above my head. I opened my eyes. I told God that I would follow the instructions that I was given when they came back to pull out the tube and if it was my time, then so be it.

The nurse came back and asked me if I was ready. I told her yes. She said, "Take a deep breath." I did and she pulled the tube out. I told her about the scenarios. She said, "The only one that you didn't see was the one about me telling you that I was going to take the tube out. He was trying to tell you that was what you needed to pay attention to." The doctor told me that my lungs were clear and that I was going to be fine. They did a swallow test later to see if I could handle fluid or soft foods. I could.

I had an IV in my neck because they had to administer several medications at one time. My neck began to swell, and it was very painful. They did a CT scan to see what was happening. I was bleeding underneath my skin. There was a large bruise. It hurt to touch it and to move my head and arms. Whenever the nurses had to roll me over, I screamed. They figured out how to move me without causing so much pain. One male nurse didn't listen to me about how to roll me. He rolled me, listened to me scream and watched me cry with no emotion on his face. He ignored me and caused the bruise to spread across my chest.

During the rest of my stay, I received visits from several doctors and nurses who treated me in the emergency room. They all said the same thing: I looked better than I did the last time that they saw me, and that the other day I looked terrible, and they did everything in their power to save me because they were not going to let me die. One of the nurses told me that they tried to put my hair up but decided that they had more pressing stuff to do so they left it alone. They braided my hair once I was stable. They did several CT scans to ensure the bleeding had stopped. I woke up on Saturday morning and didn't sleep again until Monday night; that was only for an hour.

Now comes the weird part. I would look up at the ceiling tiles, and the holes formed portraits of people. There were different ones as I continued to look at them. I asked the nurses if they could see them. Now buckle up. I saw a commercial on TV that showed some black balls on a table. At least that's what I thought I saw on television. I've never seen it again. The balls went into a hole on the side. Somehow this stayed in my mind. Every time I closed my eyes, I saw the black balls. The weird thing was that they came together to form faces. It began with my husband's cousin, then they would turn into celebrities' faces. They would be sparkly, like sequins, with clothing in shades of blue, purple, and red. The people all had long wavy hair, as if they were wearing a wig. It didn't matter whether they were male or female. After a day, I tried to think of my kittens. Well, the faces turned into cat faces, but they were evil. Now I saw humans and cats. The horrible thing was that the cats would devour the humans.

I told the doctor about everything that I was seeing, and he told me that it was normal. He told me that it would go away in a few days. I couldn't wait. It was driving me nuts. Making things worse, the person in the room beside me had an alarm going off on their phone. But the noise of it kept playing over and over in my mind, so I thought the alarm was going off every five minutes, driving me crazy. I found out later that they took eight pounds of fluid off me. I want you all to know that I didn't miss any of my dialysis treatments and no one can explain to me where all the fluid in my lungs came from. They said that one lung was completely filled and the other was almost full.

I am still not afraid to die. I read Bible verses in the morning and evening, with interpretations and prayers. One of the ones that I read while in there talked about testing God. One of the foods that they tell dialysis patients to watch is potassium. I love potatoes. I eat them. They gave me medicine that will bind the potassium so that it will come out of my body. I hate it so I hadn't been using it. I decided then that I would take the medicine so that I can freely eat the potatoes, within reason.

I found out from one of the nurses who was in the emergency room with me that MJ was there when I stopped breathing. He didn't know what was going on. I'm glad he had no idea because I don't know what he would have done driving the car by himself. Michael would probably have had an accident on his way there. He did get a speeding ticket. It breaks my heart knowing that MJ was in the room.

I am so grateful to God that He spared me and didn't let me die. It was all for this purpose. He wanted me to tell you all my story.

He is no longer waiting.

www.ingramcontent.com/pod-product-compliance
Lightning Source LLC
Chambersburg PA
CBHW071153090426
42736CB00012B/2323